Optic Verve

Also by Catherine Walsh:

The Ca Pater Pillar Thing and More Besides
Making Tents
Short Stories
Pitch
Idir Eatortha
City West

Catherine Walsh

Optic Verve

A Commentary

Shearsman Books
Exeter

First published in the United Kingdom in 2010 by
Shearsman Books Ltd.,
58 Velwell Road,
Exeter EX4 4LD

www.shearsman.com

Distributed in the Republic of Ireland by hardPressed Poetry
hpp@gofree.indigo.ie

ISBN 978-1-84861-079-8
First Edition

Cover photograph by the author.

Acknowledgements

Parts of *Optic Verve, a commentary*, in earlier versions, have been published in *Free Verse, Masthead, Default, Damn the Caesars, Longhouse*, 'in blossoms atop reeds it plows", *Origin, Radical Society, Kore* broadsheet, and the hardPressed Poetry pamphlets Pomepleat and *from* Optic Verve.
Thanks to everyone involved.

Optic Verve

A Commentary

i.m. K. OT. 1924–2007
singing

bird better hurry
yet meant should change
in stare whatever pursue
while repose as ever just
time separate effect present each way
of this never need or fulfil
not only decision it's blinded
for chance perfectly allowance
once mind

that gather know pleasure
as all as can be left for it
will stop because time now as
when can always alert in pass
just sense make it now
like what there is enough mind care
much will once nearly often there

it is not answer and custom
are whether just as all then must
difference not that only
for this morning comfort
assurance well were it anytime
just more and when better
not on all longer or in it a
gone

juntos   por la noche

ask will or must stay mind
none may lost it at most
mean by likeness ways miss for more
nearly what time which what can
establish for more seeds all can be
for which only need must be
always on think it is clear
for outwardly to regular
useless call change in can think
or ever yet well evening of tall
not less or only cloak with very
two who could and learned most
after all will wish must some
just once

con voz que ellos
conocen llamándoles

aid or like best
happened then only add to half
time one quietly might way let
it can try changed to progress if
happens all not waiting now land
hardly thought of as well means
nothing say that cry back
meant all which lightly met of
which nobody so close and
in chance

cuán hondó (cuán sin
fin

ask more with not which measure
by name as by more person do
neither best by no ours theirs
no other than exchange cause in
finally alighting at best behalf
think well express neither it is by
do not see for which hope neatly
is delight not shone can out

nunca mas
no volved nunca mas

aquí estoy

best why which can call given
away so undo better for which remember
thin with likely of which in all
only where day call and forget change
it as last could all that get
many asked no one might be just can
should be should what in all out of
neither with a glad either welcome to
known day all can who will or see
without no wonder

place curious are hold of be for
change in it was thought then
although when shortly could
this which it is let use know
better and be this then lost by
time sing of which rather
could as no one able
thought without at it happens or

as time pages no hours finishing
prepared ordinary or mostly better
why are ought known want
be given as much not could to
everything of

surcease of contact

the surcease (of contact)
"it"
   to mature in his imagination

to mature in his? imagination
— world of want and world of plenty — she was
consequently free to live, naturally —

                    un desconocido

un libro   en rústica
                haber sido engendrado

resaca   ensayista
              dramaturgo
              narrador

el y lo que es descarnado   su realismo implacable
   amargada
despojado del tiempo   de su infancia

desterrado de su tierra natal

          no me viene a la memoria
la calzada

                es un sinvergüenza
el mucho hablar

              llegaría con tiempo sobrado
saboreando el paseo
                                        acero

la tersura   apenas demarcados por setos bajos
   celo
              prolijo
                          filas

To find oneself constantly in kitchens. Bathrooms too. It does seem to predicate a sort of liking. Affinity is too strong a description, acceptance too passive, fondness too sentimental. Familiarity states the case without evoking anything of the complicated responses provoked.

Perhaps one hundred or so years ago I would have simply put my naigín of whiskey on the shelf, my pipe in my pocket and sat outside the door in the Indian Summer sunshine, scrubbing the potatoes or mending the trousers, watching the very late last blue damselflies and wasps whirr round to die. A dance macabre, hung on the solidity of an air wrapped in minute particles of dust and mould, with the wet sharp green of nettle beds, the musky odour of half-rotten tree bark in my nose.

Or perhaps I would have gone to town in the pony and trap, selling eggs or butter, buying flour, meat or sugar. The pony and trap could have brought me to teach at a school or in a private house, or visiting relations or friends at a time of extra work or need.

My maternal granny was thirteen in nineteen thirteen, the year she started boarding school, the year her father died and she finished boarding school, returning home to a governess/companion, the year of the Great Lockout in Dublin. She remembered it all vividly well into her eighties.

My own father now just turned eighty is equally at home in a landscape of a bygone era, in Dublin as a student pharmacist; pictures of him in tan khaki Bermudas and a many-pocketed flying jacket (in the seventies to us kids a 'bomber' jacket – but a real one). Small round wire-framed spectacles, hair brushed, it seems, straight up and back, already receding slightly, if spectacularly. A bicycle and a gaggle of friends lying on the grass in the background. He looks happy. Or outside a small farmhouse in Mayo, my granny seated on a súgán chair, dressed (it is the nineteen forties) in a floor-length dark skirt, a high-necked blouse, a shawl. Her stern aquiline beauty shy of his camera.

Photography had fast become a big hobby of his, once he had his first job, pre-Dublin. He took photographs, developed them and negotiated a deal with local shops so he could print batches for sale to tourists. Lighting, grain, tone, angled composition. A small Box Brownie bought second-hand at first, I think.

'Everything is the same and everything is different', N decided during the summer. Nearing eight seems to promote such pronouncements. In Spring we had 'there is really no such thing as a perfectly straight line.' Talking, questioning round these aphorisms, much like his elder brother at a similar age. I remember that feeling, excitement, discovery, speculation. The realisation that the world I knew was not a fixed unit in stasis, or the same as anyone else's. Freedom.

Tentatively, infrequently, an emergence.

Whose gift was it? To say what is my name is not tantamount to saying I don't know who I am.

Whose name was it? The gift, of course, objectively, is from a particular name to another one. Whose gift, whose name, would tell us what, significance.

The signifier applied to the signified in question, or doubt, would formulaically lead, in turn, to a speculative or possible conclusion of the matter. Which in itself, of no matter, merely waves. Respondent at the nerve ends, establishing the verification of the connective tissue would take some time.

Right by me, verging, casting shadow and too much rustle and breath is coming a man, hands on hips; "TV3 News says they've started knocking down Fatima Mansions today." "Have they?" At last, or at least. And all those people gone, or dead, or maimed in the heart of things. "They were built in 1951." "Yeah, Tom said they started when he was still studying. Before that he was cycling past fields, vegetables, cows."

How odd perhaps not to have it all there, just as usual forever, like death. Will everybody get the flat/house/maisonette they need? What will be built next? Will the quality of planning and design reflect the people's needs? Will the quality and durability of construction last even as long as the old lot? Undoubtedly it will bring its own set of hiccups. What about Oliver Bond St. and Theresa's Gardens, why don't they have such a public makeover? What will they call it? How can it not be Fatima right there, by Maryland? If there were no Luas line nearing completion (or bankruptcy) would anyone with access to power have given a damn?

Whose place was it? To say what is its name is not tantamount to saying I don't know what it is. Naming is not a speculative art and not necessary, as many seem to assume, to actual comprehension. Understanding. Naming makes communicative interaction a lot less tedious and time consuming. A coded shorthand of the specific, necessary component of the everyday dialectic of our lives.

Whose place was it? To say what its name is is saying I don't know whose it is. There's a girl somewhere, in London or Birmingham, Madrid or Barcelona, who says what its name is every time she tells her story. She says its name in her head, to hear the vowel sounds echo right; aloud they must be adapted for the pertaining local influence, to be understood, superficially.

There's a boy in Cork or Clondalkin, Amsterdam or Australia, with a history of hard times, hard work and an attitude that tells what sucks, straight off. He says the name, block and flat number in the same unpunctuated blurt, to get it over with, that he learned when he started school.

Winter. About a year ago, the junk-addicted son of a widowed flat-holder in Fatima died twisted up, wrapped in an overcoat, huddled on the doorstep of his recently deceased mother's home. Dublin City Corporation (that same one that so publicly bestows titles and accolades on the strategically needed deserving) did not recognise him as a tenant so he was locked out. Alliances. He had been living there all his life. Home.

then summer

(to be)
barefoot   lay on the
in the   step
rain   scent   rhythm and tone   you fed
                                                                                snitched
sandals in   flat   bread
(my) pocket   spatters of sycamore   biscuits
boys   back of a t-shirt
shorts   mossed   cleaned his eyes
(pockets)
indiscriminate   tangled   wavy   hurry!
beigy   fair
                                                                              put your shoes on!
light   grinning
bleached by   squinting   wash your hands!

sun   tousled   in the scullery
time   curly   dark   with the new spring water
brine   yelling
                                  sprinting   running hard
picking in home   scabs   briar
over the yards   scrapes   (she goes to the
stones   step and calls

hungry   clear   su pper
                                  voices   a calm high
the purring   carrying voice
dog   we said   for the slow air

stop the sound
              which exactly

only know

   look
break it down
steps

  that's

                    stop   this road is going
no   where can the

   signpost be   here see

way out
              by   on balcony

standing spot light hall
below
              it is tuesday   for speech

lads these saturdays a nightmare for art

                                                daft

                                                                     chart
                                                chance
                                                   choice
                                                                 chain

                                       evenings
                                                         spent
                                             suspense

brilliance   shaping conformities
                                    around a rectangular block

          angling
              current fluctuation
slow   retain necessary deposits
          for an
alluvial
fan

mid late   Dec 05   words weight
persuasion   each affirmation
wives and daughters   a value
among
poetry and prose   those   who venture
out
and here we are   style   trans
mutable   through
the 21st century   language
fails
where they've only begun
the lazy
getting round (to it   convention
apparently
ensuring its
worth   or some
C18th rationalism   such   throwback
to
v.   what?   uneven
quotidian
ignorance   the external
materialism   framework
still skeletal
—mind the gap—   scaffolding
stagnant   gap
the train sped off   every day
wearing
bending through the tunnel   tones
a   rush of   heated   vertical
structures of
air on the repetitive   power
draught   passengers
seemingly only having jumped on   defying
internalised
doors closing   a coat tail here a
squashed claustrophobic expression   ideologies
which were
there   justifying
oppression

A picture of a portrait of Charlotte

All about, that's what it could be. Encompassing, contextualizing, emphasizing, highlighting, shielding. Whose agenda? Why? Stand up! What are your reasons? Please enumerate. Their necessity? What is your first priority? Your second? Which aspects may you choose to omit? ( ) what loss to verity, this swirling narrative haze? Impressionistic as a fruit yoghurt.

Back. Reiterate. Lightening casts the sky, heavy sticks of water rain downwards, mercilessly. This in such a northern light. Grim, empty purse. Cardigans? What of them? No matter. Only the advent of cardigans as everyday items must have had some impact, not least of function, utility. Has Gradgrind been about? Hmm, he never left America. Oh you didn't know he'd gone there. Seeming to remember him in other cultures, cardigan/ubiquitous sandwich, overcoat/ulster/wellington. What is the question?

That is the question. Trying, revealing to a child, a child. What needs to be asked here, at this juncture? Here, at this? Why? How will that pertain to the outcome? Is there an outcome? How else term whatever consequence is then? Did you understand anything more or differently? Did you meet, what?

A picture. Not a photograph, perhaps a photograph. Not a painting, perhaps a painting. A print, an engraving, an etching, a drawing in pencil or charcoal. One has occasion to wonder. And to wonder does that, in the least, matter. A portrait. Not a snap, maybe improvised. Not a photograph, maybe a photograph, etc. I got tired of that one. We were approaching the mid-nineteen-seventy song lyric there, with terrifying abandon.

A picture of a portrait, Charlotte. Of Charlotte, a picture. A portrait, Charlotte. A of a; a Charlotte of a portrait. Charlotte of a picture. Charlotte of a picture of a portrait. It's not even tennis on a blue court, nor those strangely elongated days beyond the new building (no longer), built over since. Hedged round, beautifully sheltered, a tad neglected, overgrown. Dipping nets, old-fashioned, scuffed, hard surface. A heavy, wooden-framed tennis racquet that seemed unduly large. Dragging back home, bag, racquet, two buses; the never-diminishing wait. Kelly's Corner, observers' paradise, delight. Affable Middle Eastern shop owner who had children cross to shelter under the awning in heavy showers, extending it over the concrete slope for them. We were not likely to be carting home sacks of rice and beans unaided. Struck each time he did this that he did not need to make the offer. Later he would have fruit, vegetables, saving 5p till I got there, picking something fresh. The occasional very hot day giving elderly women carrying shopping a seat, a glass of water, he would ask if we would like to wait beneath the awning. This was part of beginning to notice meeting other peoples, other cultures.

cid
so many
seams
altered
states
4 homes
4 years
7 in 8
how many
changes
my
curtains
take

many
seams
altered
states
4 homes
years
7 in 8
some
changes
blinds
take

There is
something
arid
peculiar
the barren
wayside
warping
the dull steel
barrier
a
quality of
day
light
in unexpected
eyes

There
is
something
arid
peculiar the
barren
wayside
warping the
dull
steel

quality
of
days
lights
unexpected
eyes

is it   revelatory   form   small
sketch   incarnation   the range
contributing   or textured white   with
chillies   the common object
    metaphysics an   outdated anomaly
captivating an unwieldy accusation ah when
meant something   by the time he was
being exuberant memories drifting enthrallingly
after the war   a   finished machinery
frozen ideas   packets troubled by a
beautiful melancholy   in   conversation
comedy is a play   showing   the
moment to bite upon   comes one
of the   first   shambolic forgiveness to
provide   considerably in vogue expect a story pervade

boat
out
no sail up
yet
some
breeze
fishing
lines cast
hard
lean poles
twitch bend
scales of
repetitive
movement
chorus of
laughter
voices
thrown across
(dawn)
bay
early
(day)light
shaded lamps
hazed
controlling
perspective

imagine if you could have done all
that without ever having to
leave home impossible of course one
only conjures the outcome the impetus
some trajectories omits what
so much of us live everyday
anywhere whichever way you pretend
it did or didn't happen there is a
necessary hiatus valve perhaps imagine
if you could without ever having to have
done all that only conjures leave home one
impossible of course the impetus omits the
outcome what some trajectories much of us
live everyday what so whichever it did or
didn't there is a way you pretend
anywhere hiatus happen perhaps
imagine valve if you could imagine if
you could all have done that having to
ever without impossible leave of course
home one only conjures the outcome some
what omits the trajectories what impetus
everyday imagine so much of us live
whichever way anywhere of course the
impetus it did or didn't happen if
you have home of course without ever
having to pretend the outcome omits some
trajectories imagine so everyday much of
us happen

is
making do?
day is
boys play
boy fight
(no, we are arguing…)
exhaust falls
off the car
again
hat
left behind
chair
loaded
with books
turn off the
light
day
bright
hailstorm

sound of wooden
houses all around
site
specific

trying not to watch
the methodology
all new and

untried
in a bog
are we mad
yes
/ tired crazy
stopping to
hold on
by a riverbank
iron-age stronghold
in the mossy air
remains

Niall's morning nap, Tallaght
we all live round here
this time day quiet gardens
blossoming birdsong half filled
bin bags rattling distant / voices
interiors soaking out open
window; clattering delph clanking
pans most small children
sleeping now he's out red-blue
pyjamas blue socks dragging a small
electric lawnmower by the flex up
down the road
tricky junction stopping to play
with litter feed his horse
some/don't ya know they both try to
drink from the hollow handle
centre of a rectangular drain
lid / it is a hot day he is very fair
turning purple he is looking
for food examining rubbish
with delicate sniffing discarding
trekking many roads / similar junctions
several blocks picking grass from unknown
gardens chewing slowly no spitting
doesn't touch Stewart's sourbellies
young dandelion leaves how could he
know? maybe two and a half if three he's
left a lot / this time
day quiet gardens blossoming birdsong
scattering cadences across backs of houses
spades footballs sandbuckets scooters angled on
grass   smell of cooking sleeping
children wakening quiet gardens blossoming
birdsong lunch having their shoes put on

at least
easy violin careers
faultlessly

the very stepped this is not
meshed interwoven
hearing this voice
saying weave be quiet not a weave
annoys listen not a weave
carefully formulated sequence of series
why? / is there a poet who?
painter of light?
there are tunnels
all want more / (money) listening to watching
the thinking
have realizing i am lucky yet not
fruit vegetables making shapes subdued
light curtained doorway
wire baskets underpinning otherwise vacuous
untenable structural assembly
—walking into light pictures road edging on—
village to bridge
which has been decapitated rebuilt to accommodate the
new luas train

or another yeuch
no matter what sayings doings you conclude conclude
deduct conclude world terribly intact box-like parameters exist
specifically walling up call it supporting elision
of any natural good sense processed packaging of eagerness curiosity
quick commodification arrogance attempting dominance
lots of people to ask to leave the enclosure------

page 6 in a triangle
on the back   through
beech leaves   playing
the base metal with air
vibrating till sound forsook
its distinct parts
took over   ceasing along the
other side of something
( )   heard as silence
an other   no noise
other   quiet
an other   still
or surroundings   vibrating
air   with the base metal playing on
the back   through beech leaves used
to be all else like   a catch   precision
staving off literate descriptions   2 or 3
together   bypass an attempt   or   beginning
mid tone
        only if heard in
scale   condemned
to cyclical   repeat
process   annihilate   regard
patterning
              perceptions
      desire

where
are long
why have day
my boots short
skirt
they cold
been wind
left
behind walking
it’s no good
fast
smiling
at away
now i’m turning
me
blue
still you
i see

continuity
what
lies beneath
granite
outcrop
bog butter iron
age cluster
hill fortification
on the rises
in the valleys
dell river
thin blanket
unproductive bog
covered so
urban
cnoc moín a lín

<pomepleat>

bracketing
[lives

scales
chain
mailed
eyes held
wide
open by
will
power
see
next?

gyrating on the
line
stumbling over
thresholds
balancing in doorways

of tremendous
towards
a spherical light
depth stretching
focus
over
points stasis
evanescent barely
perceptible
movement

some
difference opined

heard nothing
but tiny
shiftings shuntings
cracklings driftings
saw nothing
but shapes round
ball
bouncing curves on
an inclined plane
towards
a meniscus

called sky
pliable
interlocking

a term
life

these marks   we make
hold in mind
ear heart brain   for you
to take   us   to
understand

whorl
leaf
vein
snail
shell
hoar
frost
a directing
of desire

selection
of matter

interpretation
of events
or is that
intent?

whorl
leaf vein
snail shell
hoar frost
a directing
of desire

selection
of matter

interpretation
of events
or is that
intent?

thumbnail
sketch

<\pomepleat>

that's three different tapes citing run away as the only solution reactionary predicated on an idealism involving complete inaction it couldn't get much worse could though the trying pretending oscillating nerves and the whining nasal high-pitched drone of the newer   less than doesn't come into it in the city on the outskirts in the fields with seasonal clouds of mobile phone bearing quad bike riders counting the sheep both literally and metaphorically though presumably not both in the same place at the same time all things being dependant on their source their environs their raison d'etre and whoever is in charge of the purse strings probably a variety of flexi and this is always looking at the bright side of the street where the grass is and there is no pie but look lets say the slugs had completely deserted the garden only aphids larvae ladybirds earthworms and preferably a dearth of horseflies and wasps thank you what difference would that make no need for salt and good beer down jamjars   what difference the perfectly realized mrs so and so just so so leant lightly on the wall   in passing   resting her umbrella on the brickwork wasps crawling over the handle in profusion is there a sting   in that   i could not say   she moved along quite self-consciously   retrieving her umbrella carefully as she went till at last the butterflies were out i had been waiting for them lost in thought for   possibly   days   i no longer looked to see had she successfully denied the burgeoning wasp rave their transport   or even to notice had any other leg stepped into the frame   watching the low level desperation for some years now   these are the external contexts when will it come over me like a climatic warp   can I leap quite high enough at all fast enough to prevent being moidered in the fall out of the game in which i wish as always to have no part slap the door claps back lightening streaks across the floor realizing the grain hand-picked motes   electricity charging   a sliding cushion to fall blue   as the scale   lifts stairs   the percussive influence of doors auditory vibration in the hollow houses is your voice any nearer to my voice because you like to play there is an imposition along the lines of   pretending you are not in a monologue for the sake of art in the 21st century   don't you like writing   if one does engage in such at all   what's the point if no point attaining a wonderfully lyrical witty caustic cue   for whomsoever feels like it moody   lost a series of climbing cadences waffling out a patio door like tuesday as the milkman can't count keeping tally by the big lake how many did you see   we will go back and count again or we will go back and not bother to count at all ever that's best for resuming returning moving dancing tripping by the cyst grave farther crossing over along under the stand of beech trees as the rain plops flatly above us and dribbles off the wide ribby leaves whose sandwiches are they i'm not eating that he licked it you did i saw you and your nails are filthy well what did you expect no you spat in my bottle of water i don't care i can hold my mouth up to the sky what will you use to filter the midges out ha ha think you're so clever my teeth then i can pick them off no that is disgusting 'snot it's improvisation 'sthat right catherine that word

wooden floored sunny sittingroom
            light floes   white
voile rolled bamboo   shadowed lines

black ochre arm chairs
blue tape   measure crosses floor
halfway
line established correctly   small
marla figures with
football compete   pitch
score sheet   set time   lego goals   continues
polishing floor   socks pants sweatshirt
     hair
upstairs   (like)   moving
    house room tidying vacuum
  cleaning furniture shunted loudly
   dropped footsteps clattering wood
                washing machine
slurping   then
reasonably characterize
                                                  puerile
  wit too

does it bother me   perhaps
apparently not nearly so much
[as you]
      now who said that?   (this time
it has become tedious
who can   (how   when why)
thousands of potential combinations
              knowing it otherwise would
                              have been differently tedious
and   ,   that time,   hellish

if time wrong
      now who said that? this time
      now who said that? that time
time wrong

wrong time   if is
or was   maybe could be equally
       now who said that? this time
who can   how   when why
thousands of potential combinations
      if is   or was   does bother me
apparently not nearly so much
[as (it does) you]
      [now who] said that

That day having had to say to myself, she to herself, you've thought of something, write it down. The sort of instruction usually saved for irritants, trifling areas of conflict between family members, classroom groups, the we-have-moved-beyond-signposting role, self-assigned or adopted, adapted in default, yes, the door is open, so somebody close it. Simple, never ceasing to be irritated, exasperated at the propensity for conflict in differing areas of everyday life; bickering, bitching, moaning. As had been written elsewhere — that such should be the dominant cacophony sounding ostentatiously, vociferously, round so much social life in any direction, was a shame. Such a banner slapping in the wind, one couldn't miss it. Presumably updated, generalized versions of an béal bocht. We've always moaned, bitched, whined, had a huge chip on our collective shoulder, so we're bloody well not going to stop now attitude. So there. Aren't we great. Trouble is, it turns off, social interactions, ideas, activities. Dead-end tennis, slap in the face both ways, always looking for some one/thing to blame. In localized regional pockets many children still brought up in the guilt culture, necessarily the blame culture. State of mind, stagnation of attitudes becoming vitrified with time.
Easy writing too much, easy writing too little. Easy saying hell! What constraints! Not writing at all. Not easy to live with. As Winnie-the-Pooh or dinner, respectively, what goes up/in must come down/out. However transformed, in what modality. Is this perhaps the intellectual groundwater for W.B.'s eventual distancing into an evanescent twilight irradiating the occasional beauty, the odd insight, the moral or ethical tag of the times?
We all but reflect our culture.
That is a nicely ambiguous piece of literacy which actually carries it. Amorphous, and, well, bald.

an impositional narrative
what other kind
                exists
its implication of
authorship   authority   absolutism
        logicity   geometrical
contortions
(seeming unaware
(of risking)
these displays   however elongated
wherever   shaped
whomsoever   parades
carnival
certainly carefully accessed formulated
even practiced   in effect
part of the display   nonetheless
history bleeding hearts
purported put about by
few for many   tiny percentage
draw a graph   as for
development of a child's growth
percentile chart   ...
place the countries of the world according
to economic power   military
power   academic power
media power   / blah

the light times in the west
political typewriter
swerving
swerving through night
swerving alright
largely uncollected
great unbought
wind factor
the futility door
          — trenchcoat and turbine —
poows   swoop
implicit leaving
relinquishments
abandonments   in that very spot
abandontherun   ar an láthair seo
abandon the run   i láthair daoine
                                                  surrounded by people

          4 books on it
          leabhar
as láthair

now none   / all
happening the happened   as láthair   absent
out of service/no   signposted   from never was

will the next publisher please step forth

excruciating moment of light

they ask me what i remember
so i feel my feet stick in flat, strapped Clarke's sandals,
to rising bubbles of tarmac along the road to   , i hear
the crack as i pull my foot off breaking the shiny skin — smell
of heat on the road, small rectangular bales of hay drying
other side of the ditch   where we find over the course of summer,
wild strawberries, raspberries, blackberries, — small sweet
fruit entangled in briars, suckers, small birds flash   flutter
along their line   cross the road   flying low in front to
land in the ditch
acres of flax   sugarbeet   corn   barley   oats   wheat
fields of potatoes
sheep grazing   cows mooching over the land
      the quiet persisting river

always a pleasant surprise finding it met with huge you are the
generation easy money/venerable festive bright things the group's
plenty at their peaks you seem condemned/is that released it's
live to be launched garishly musical years ago sadly unnecessary
creatively crazy as a stylistic tenet or virtue drab in-house obsessive
of abstruse/features living behind buttons sensors censoring since the
testament beset by a poor/frame rate cleverly all those with scenes
complemented contemporary settings the/man with the number one
haircut the woman with the rings and the lit cigarette/ queuing up past
substitutes enemies enhancing light staying put debauchery in the/
middle of your body moving tougher new nights large hats adhesive
strips have/floundered expansively comes up deep a nerve touch flair
for irreverence she says/irrelevance i say there here choreographed
a film staged as an event now then it bore/the anxiety of currency
designed to bring a bit of what captures vibrancy highly individual
traceries candid warts and all there they are as ever up for grabs down
and/out a line in the soup kitchen cardboard home on the street dole
queue on a wet/miserable pox of a day a disease recently people as
symbols our media a blight a/candid honesty reminiscent of some
perfectly placed asylum perplexing procedural/take on the madam

there is an interesting question on anarchy but hope springs eternal
perfectly lookout/too how should we promise more the coat is inside
out you say other truncated and/following costly regrettably hyped
and blurbed conducted to the heights of/paddywhackery but also
suspected of involvement with the nudist burble of the/commedia
dell'arte offering presence a role space permitting or simply homage
to/prime or process procedure or an assemblage contorting style
to the most close/resembled thrill ate involvement and combined
headphones with a hearty physique/this could be a bawdy tale instead
we are promising you an extraordinary one which is/enacting itself
all around as you already have perceived/any level of interest is/
hundreds of people a week remixed and labelling lots of pretty bleak
forgettable sad/all over new york newry boston ballyhaunis barcelona
ballymun paris piedmont/kilkenny knightsbridge and as for the babies
apparently women have never truly/absorbed and formulated the
experience before or not in the public domain as a person/looking
sporadically and only slightly backwards at skewed angles from a

moving/vehicle might give a fantastically distorted version of events from such an enclosed/delimited perspective.

Level of vindictive vainglory   factory churnout   sheep in the machine precisely/what choices did you make, actually, in hard reality, altered your child's birth, made/you as independent as possible, put you in charge, informed and unafraid of this basic biological process always a pleasant surprise finding it met with huge you are the/generation easy money venerable festive bright things the group's plenty at their/ peaks you seem condemned is that released it's live to be launched garishly musical/years ago sadly unnecessary creatively crazy as a stylistic tenet or virtue drab in-house/obsessive of abstruse features living behind buttons sensors censoring since the testament beset by a poor frame rate cleverly all those with scenes complemented/ contemporary settings the man with the number one haircut the woman with the rings/and the lit cigarette queuing up past substitutes enemies enhancing light staying put/debauchery in the middle of your body moving tougher new nights large hats adhesive/strips have floundered expansively comes up deep a nerve touch flair for irreverence/she says irrelevance i say there here choreographed a film staged as an event now then/it bore the anxiety of currency designed to bring a bit of what captures vibrancy/highly individual traceries candid warts and all there they are as ever up for grabs/down and out a line in the soup kitchen cardboard home on the street dole queue on a/wet miserable pox of a day a disease recently people as symbols our media a blight a/candid honesty reminiscent of some perfectly placed asylum perplexing procedural take on the madam

must have been like a   you have no idea
caged lion she said   I said as
line bipped   echochamber effect impeded
decibel level rose a steady graded roaring attempt
at clarity   comprehension   efficacy   where would we
be without this long line coiling continents countries
counties   desolate inappropriate
then finally   quality
whose philosophical elements   history I put some
this is what   where   is past
opinion   the fact of   noun
the only thing   the activity of gerund
is how it is   inevitable
animated   criticism of
establishment   a particular
beliefs   kind
although substantial   nothing posited
you make one   nothing gained
position dominant   raise your aim
conviction   the futurity of
dropped shifted   these ill-defined
picked up   places
a facility   in their preordained
particularly   modalities
guiding the reader   the village
on the other hand   truly
an instance of   gone
inability   to leave
there could have been   a hegemony
                                                 an open space
more said   across which race
advantage as women   expanded
of the workforce   better benefits
enables   children to school;
a fact   facilitates
in the service sector   represented
significantly   no change
    manufacturing   generally

before i know these things i will not see

years after   they shared a
glass   lodged   moved boulders
by osmosis   came in out
the same front door   times
together   times separately
wariness of draft   returning so
many   80s emigrants   these years

i used to say   this
predicament   none   of which
no matter constructed where various
followers   deny their workers
recognised him   imagination
extraordinary   a more specific
attempt   the centre   maintained
the ability   considered   it's true
did   i dream   does it matter
in the Big Diningroom my
grandmother's mother's memories
in our limited senses   delicacy
comfort   skilled maintenance   a tenacious endurance
is the product   they say   yes
they   mouthing inadequacies
forms of repression frozen
decades centuries elsewhere the
language of regression shored up
under authoritarian banners
of liberation movements liberating
forces hardly a misnomer while a
contradiction in terms misinformed workers
abused workers regimes running on
the poverty of masses the
ignorance of underdeveloped
mind   fears   difference
identity politics   needing redressing
readdressing   soundbites

aromatic farts lingering
insubstantial attention seeking
unproductive environmental
fouling in the guise
of fair play
an inherent nature

this
rattled
subjectivity
I I I hear
you you
say

as I (too)

read
your (possessed)
poetry
why
so
many
feelings
for
what
reason
do you
cease

listening
only
observe waters
course
gradients in
the ear sounds

i i i here
you you
say
hear
say

as i to
read
you're (possessed)
poetry
why so
many feelings
for
what reason
do you
cease

you cease
listening only
observe
waters

course

action

take
a
word
replete

exhibiting
obscurely
and begins   journey
sudden
sparks   light
was
a question
asked   to remember
moments
of
astonishing   in these
respects
plodding uphill
bareness   lips pursed   persistently
there
were
clouds
flashed
light
window
shook   orchard
never
had   a gate
aged
damson tree was   marking way up a ditch
river
village / hamlet / straggle of farms
place of occupying force
farm home   home

on the road
still

high wide
hand
understand
away
ancient gardens
wake up
happening
head full of
immensities
world small
again
expansive
stretchy
encompassing

sketchy
life

Whose small drafts were they amongst the litter debris of
responsibility looming crumbs butterdish miscellaneous novels
biographies sheets of oddly sized strangely assorted papers biro
Tipp-Ex and marmalade dish the intrusive radio transmitter of the
pulpit i am the epitome of authority in my chosen field/anything
i care to fling my hat at voice the unbelievable lack of ability to
cohere to pronounce to be stylistically or hey lets not ask for too
much even grammatically cohesive you are on the radio broadcasting
i cannot see you that is what you have not learnt to make credible
or interesting why back out of the air to the undeniably solid
table replete with when did i have the chocolate bar was that with
the coffee which had followed up the decaf knowing full well the
mug of tea and glass of water had preceded the journey out this
morning seeming really quite far away when thinking when not
prone to nervousness lethargy serial boredom overlaying mundane
chores which oh they have sent your letter that is mine to you back
where are you now with how many children seem to remember
hearing two anyway serial chores in other instances provide vitality
rhythm dynamo brakelights still tired of the whingers semi-
professional begrudgers moaners enormous cultural gap low level
of language usage not only do some things not change this has
definitely increased abysmal lack of vocabulary intonation patterns
grammatical structures evident preschoolers no difficulty seeing
those having continuing language problems showing signs of specific
learning styles/needs by 4 or 5 developing gaps requiring individually
tailored assistance for 3 or 4 years lots of 1 to 1 to bridge those ever-
growing hiatuses by 8 did it all happen course not most obvious
worst cases evidencing severe behavioural difficulties eventually
get minimal help when the department can be induced to provide
the funding persuaded all necessary qualifying criteria fulfilled it is
not good enough to change curriculums not good enough pushing
policies of integrated inclusive schools systems without providing
the wherewithal to perform these tasks our educational system like
our health system struggling to stand still while we badly need new
hospital buildings extra wards look at crumlin, we also need lots of
new school buildings all over the country, no region county should
take precedence, large airy multi-purpose constructions allowing
for the ever-changing demands of running schools, adequate sturdy

clean toilet facilities separate wash up facilities for art and craft
and to allow children wash hands before eating, clean sealed well
maintained waste disposal bins, recycling bins, seating appropriate
in size to average age, more whiteboards, flip charts, overhead
projectors, computer screens, fewer blackboards, reasonable break
and lunchtime supervision indoors and out, choice of activities
indoors and out at these times to suit all ages abilities, a healthy food
campaign actually put into practice having a fruit or good food break
in the morning, sadly could go on and on and on so much room for
improvement in the general everyday welfare of children at school

when one   their object   turned-up
restore her an unusual number of
people to an obscure   paragraph
        just noticing unironic why
is   awful   brilliant shocked
darkness   with a jump   single
twist   slope slackened   happening
really   cliff-edged with
savage dread heavy afternoons
beyond animation unnaturally
hidden   no   one   passed realize
there is no frame clipping
    pioneers un-ideal it was all
he could find   say curiosity
nothing has had surroundings
jolted for instance light
fixtures for plumbing after
day showed on their faces
not quite met   failing to
discuss in consequence also
energetic wan in progress
now set close garden
orchard will have to wait just
over an ambiguous leaning on
the wall   nothing   took her in sense
of attention perhaps   lagging so come
to at least half the point
regretting attrition meaning that
evening did not see us who
could turn their heads on the
road   hope crippled by
rhetoric we could advertise
characters cavorting essential
corner of behaviour released
why are   they   here   discomfort

makeshift   sky   suppose it all
happened again decided not to
walk   past   this place there's no
one here   remarked have a laugh
pause   crowds absorbed by
  light   taken   over by food
subsumed in   continuous holding
circles   radioactive waves
   energy   it was not good
these angry unhappily   hard
to remember why pronounced so
ineptly   clutching the faster
  faster he knew whispering who had
gone noisy of   unwritten   to
compete with similarly you see
part of   trembled   grabbing
so much effort we turned off
the stars in your past earth
sandy retain the journeys helpless
where   this   no more than a few
yards   activity and grey   what came
do you remember the animals and
birds   it was unlikely   the
question interesting   in a book
   took me so many years
symptom like bad grace legs
luxury served up preachy not
necessarily having an easy time
here stopped i went out
     but   groaning
tired   overwhelmed   this long
conversation tilted talking

or investigating sleeping
humorous i thought that
intending what did you want to
how can you say those like
recordings we never made bypassed
showing our teeth harmlessly in
the sideways zenith of the 5th
erogenous zone or was it i been
talking about you know how often
we slept out everyone knew
he laughed lightly that's who
you didn't block it
nothing remember well his eyes
what do you
mean life/and everything challenge/
if you like me i
can walk carry my bag
look after myself noticeably
to a list surprised down the
years stranger
company faced with this
repetitive working hard
the past a sense where i
quickly got out fly was
watching night useless
point smells of place
neglected in a shirt still
distanced from his head
shoulders peculiarly i wished
i was there seeing point
now as clearly then wait
uncut grass people wanting
talk moving through nebulous
apertures sniffing rooting true

themselves   i stopped   without
being   overheard   night sky
mirror   and   microphone
i was gone
the art of catoptrics of
light   play the
thaumatrope   ah but now how
show   to imagine life
sight   before   pre 1827
linear narration only
or   parallel literary time
or merging moments scenes
abandoning their moment for each
other proceeding into the next view
i do like sitting down   writing
such a morning   high
clouded strong autumnal sunlight
themselves   i stopped   without
being   overheard   night sky
mirror and
where i was gone
art of catoptrics of
light play the
thaumatrope   ah   but now how
show   imagine   life
sight before   1827
linear   narration only
/   parallel   literary   time
/   merging moments scenes
abandoning their moment for each
other proceeding into   next view
i do like sitting down   writing
such a   morning   high
clouded strong   autumnal   sunlight

at that archaeological site
on the right of the monaleen road
down past the national school
on the way to sandville cross
just in to your right there when
you've passed the green beside monaleen park
underneath that new road

the archaeologist said that what
mr. healy's 4th class and the other
older children at monaleen national
school saw this morning will
be covered with a new road
by the end of this week

a fortification   a round house
cremated bones in urns older than
the settlement as they were found
under their bank a broken skull
of a woman of around 40 years old in the
trench around the house   pre christian
late celtic   a ripe old age
charcoal   pottery   an iron knife   blade intact
a whetstone   a thumb scraper for curing
hide   and the ubiquitous and much more
recent   bowl of a clay pipe   mark intact

were the two children and adult
in the urn burial   accompanied
by their pet   or were those
the bones remaining from some
kind of feast/funeral
how many people lived there?
twelve   twenty?   what did they
cultivate   on the hilly slopes
around them?   did they build small
enclosed field systems on the slopes
like the ones in evidence on the side of the hill

by lough gur?   what did they grow?   what
animals were about?   there would have
been wild wolves   did they have
domestic dogs?   would they have
fished along the mulcair?   did they
know or trade with the people who lived
at the site found by ballysimon?   what
did they hunt?   what will their midden
tell us about dinner   bread   and their
manner of dining?   and how much of
what we can know is verifiable
through finds at this site or cross referenced
with other sites' results   how much is
speculation?   wonder   when the
bright night sky was cinemascope   inspiring awe
                              showing stories as shape   light
                                                                  movement
wonderworld beyond the tangible   for
interpretation   reinterpretation   each
        succeeding generation   earth   untouched for
possibly four and a half thousand years   we
walked there
                        now it's air

a set of four   a set of six   a set problem   then regardless
of number do i have rodents or birds in the chimney   why is there
nobody else whose job it is to come and fix it   is this where i must
be the grown up again   doesn't it stop   shouldn't it you know
a work break   respite that kind of thing   it all started such a
long time ago   when I was about four   perhaps earlier   it came
with reason   intruding into my social instinct

your
    iridescent
              glass
freezing
          nights
  pure green
yellow

all the moving
i think it is true   [what is that

whole episodes
epochs
are   not retained
in any conventional
memory
but one day
years later a
line road   resonates   triggers
incidents places people
reverberate memory

[what is   that

all the moving   i think it
is true   [what is that i lost
many clumps blots   issues events
incidents   retaining a more intangible
evidence   tricks of   light
shape of   tree   sound
of certain   leaves falling   certain surfaces
profiles   memory
landscapes in which   to create/recreate
experience   as comprehensively as   senses
allow for
understanding

grange day light snow
wind sky bird night
    river
        abhann   oíche
eán   speír   gaoth
   sneachta   solas   lá   an ghrainseach

where did these words come
from?
proto what?
is this a series of articulated
sound the youngster hoeing the
small enclosed tillage would have
recognized
would not have run from

la pesca nadando
  un arbol negro
abajo de un cielo
gris   la hierba de una
primavera tenue
amarilla, un azul verdoso,

el campo vacio
sin el cabello

los niños
dentro de sus juegos
 los libros
los dibujos

la musica del invierno

las cabezas llenan
 de pensamientos   palabras
el dia

  cantando la via
la guitarra grande
tocado por los manos
pequeñitos

y el piano
viejo
que ellos tocan

si yo pudiera
  cambiar

el mundo
      Si yo pudiera
  cogerlo
y agitarlo
  bien

      y cuando
miro

      las copas

de nieve

    pasando

flotando

    en la brisa

las cositas
  que dejan

blancas
silenciosas

    sobre
las tejadas
    de las
montañas

    siento

algo raro

las cositas
blancas

    que dejan

en el

mano

las montañas
    cubiertias

mas cerca
      de aqui

y la luna
  que no se
puede tocar

      luz

  en el mano

(por) una vez

  ceguera pasajera

      a causa

del resplondor

      de la nieve
por todo

taking one word

isolation shifts

meaning less

context juxtapose

yr board work
the
sent him to
and running

all along the
pattern recognition

skips kinship

proximity a

migration criteria
perhaps less important
quantitively
to the family than
to trade

industrial and political
challenges
privilege or progress
procedural
participation
technical goals
ownership so much

the poems of
the muses
continual
arcadia
song comedies
the space
of analogies
realism after
a test hour
tragedies
past
we didn't mean
to the last
go off go ahead
on the trail
secret water
odes boats beyond

tales complete plays
in the morning
lesser light
target choice
keys and records
mind only
the sea along
road coast

of most whispering

access any change
to write dictionaries
play hide and seek
know what to look for
in winter follow the
shores of any lake or

gets back to that reservoir lost in lush
what is held berrying is
in common what is the pond an ideal
ambience
not public and private shattered
demesne era of adhesive
liberal change threats
to pattern on physical
response if not outwards
then upwards
drifts of apertures on the
seagulls path
not voice worn dismal
sound ripples mistake the
nothing in the world aisling and colour
today in a first reading
is happen tempos in the path of
follow with still christmas the book
have at night of stories fantastic and
a head cannot more questions and answers
shake it's somebody's big show
great my little
film poster treasury of illustrated by
the complete

or would have to continue to draw along goad provoke
arrogance and hauteur impressive so many modes the priority
of an artistic self and its importance to mind in a
world before ever actually beginning to get near
producing something then the long long way to seeing if any
of it would ever really be yours to give to throw out
to disdain

al-jabr restoring
process of moving
the subtracted over

al-muqabla comparing subtracting
equally
whichever side you're on
it comes from
completing balancing

or the inheritor

when the sun is 19 degrees below
the horizon

twilight
gauging the atmosphere
a depth
unverified
until space exploration

aware of gravity's existence
with depth stretching his
vision extends emerging

optically
philosophically
immeasurable mensuration
in the estimation of
beauty

al-khwarizimi
ibn al-haytham

read page one
again

time null and void
abstract and achievable
the decision to measure
natural phenomena and their
affects on/against other natural
phenomena including ourselves
humans

negative positive
minus plus
before after
past
now future
finished
just happening
about to
yet to occur
flexible stance
elastic balance
all seeing eye
straight refraction
give and take
tension to hang
actions from
moments of occurrence
the balance of of

moments occurrence
now as a thing althing
moment as action
second as pause
or effect
then as causal
or empty finished
(the balance implicit in my leaving there)

[The Gull   August 1979

soaring upwards
  on the breeze
    wings outstretched
      curving gliding
        ducking crests of waves
      towards a horizon long blue
-sand sea sun sky
            me

Song for myself
  (Space)   Containers   1984–86

I am wind and sea
white froth on
crashing brine

I am the sleek
  sharp rock there
puddling spray

I am the seagull
  live in his cry

circling the rock
drenched in sea spit

I am the moment
his feet tip stone

I am the wings
that quiver air

I am the balance
implicit in his
leaving there]

zero to go
minus   through nothing
to plus   in addition
subtracting time
zero

what is a big word?

Unusual way of turning the log slowly. Fine tuning, bereft. Emotionless exactitude. Exhorting platitudes from the weary. Resourceless montage crossing in front of her/his eyes, passing animated expression. Passing. For. Animated. Expression.

See. That's what I mean. Mean what you see. Dubious, brief, entirely pointless; if hungry, bereft of cash, time strapped or soused, inevitable, ensuing dross. As the dynamic wavers, shifts, pacing tilts, lifts allowing it to slide off more, exactly. Pixel by pixel. Intent, meaning, evident departure.

Take off, peak, land, resume. Bite back. No my children did not devour, somehow, my life, as it had already been existing in me, quite intact and steady, long prior to any concept of them or they of it. Neither after, did they seem to seek to obliviate me, rather to be quite intrinsically, vehemently independent, each in their own right. From an early, articulate age; separate entities, entirely. Yet capable of communal life, at ease, evolving talents, skills individually, single-mindedly, haphazardly, resolutely, dynamically, funnily, enragingly, engagingly.

Unusual way, of turning the log slowly, watching it burn. Feeling dry heat reach feet, spread, disperse. Dissipated thread. Evening lilts on, limping through its slow air. Punishing schedules. Boredom. Relief. Satisfaction. That's there. I am still quite surprised at how much fighting there is, in general. Most trivial exchanges replaced by self-aggrandising aggression. That's not a chip on the shoulder it's a big mac.

Plugging. On. Plugging. In. Plugging. Out. Plugging. Along. A book on...

Brandizement.   Brandizeiamenting...

Least said...

at [which] dehumidifier enters the audioscape, sensing a certain curling, squiblike, phut-phutting downwards.

Sounds like engine failure.

Unleashing aromatics to the quilt, indeed realia. Relationship/s rule/s, write books. Don't be too cold, wet, hungry, tired. If sick, get well. If well, get on with it. If painting, resume. If fed up, retire. If restless, move something/one/where. Exploring notions cauled by the unquestioning, the unenquiring. Which is... I have been in more mindful bus queues, tarjeta at the ready. Punch click a political arena, the demography shaken not stirred. Can the solution be suspended without requiring another element? Holding area.

Contexts change perspectives. Language scaffolding the landscape. Again.

How long have you been there? Did I see you like a bump in the wall, all those same words, contextual, elemental landscape. Visual parameters set by the mind's eye. Questioning the form but not the substance. Heretical. Hierarchical patronomical incline. Haul the rope, pull up the drawbridge, formatting that slippery slope. Chute to? An integral corral perhaps, not integrity. A windowless purblind i spot. Literally, salvage yard. Rolling stock. Destination end of the line. Did I mention the turntable?

Such concerns seem knitted to uncertainty. A Fair Isle Aran being both possible and impossible. Introducing probability ratios somehow slackens the pace without actually unpicking any stitches. Writing longer equations futile, simple transference.

OK, futile but fun occasionally. Lightens the chipped firelight. It's colder. Old days gone forever (begrudging, whining platitudinous remark/refrain). I know she said it had never been her intention, nevertheless, years later, looking through the hollow tube towards a light source inevitably catches some of the multitudinous reactions of her sometimes whimsical, always haphazard decision-making process. Perhaps turning the same hollow tube excruciatingly slowly while viewing the ensuing internal chaos, colourful, beautiful, wild, original, yet still always conforming to the laws of nature, the pressures of its confines, is an indication, a hint of what goes on.

A tone of sombre light glinting colourfully, invitingly paradoxical prisms. If you could be content looking through that tube, I would leave you there. Enough changing minutely, vicariously, according to circumstances to keep your attention, alleviate your gaze.

Why should there be a resolution? Is making an effort just too trying? Therewith, an example of coyness found to be, in air or on paper, too cloying. Sticks too much together to go fast enough for the dynamic spin required. Analogy with those vitamin/mineral supplements purporting to be both good for you and attractive/tasty while leaving a lingering metallicism on the back of the tongue. The notion that while it is all that it seems, it is not fulfilling its promise in the desired manner. It is, after all, just all that it seems. Linguistic tropes, dust motes, what gauge riddling your tilth today?

Punning, a social art form. Once accustomed to expert purveyors of the pun diurnally, spoilt for life at any distance from them. That town Dublin hoarded caches of punners, they stood around bus stops on stormy days, queued for the dole in Thomas St., Werburgh St., Victoria St., pinched their fruit on Camden St., bought potatoes off prams, scrubbed doorsteps on their knees and put Grannies out on them minding babies, shelling peas, peeling potatoes, darning socks, knitting jerseys, at ease. Needed. Looked after, necessary. Full of lore and sometimes Guinness, brandy or port (smell of port makes me gag, previous, hot port, phlegm, blocked eustachian tubes, cloves. It's instant).

Grannies with quick wits, sharp minds, indeed occasionally, loud mouths. Grannies in aprons with old aluminium pans balanced on their laps, reining in the go-boys, running verbal rings around them deftly, loudly, briefly. Effectively. Keeping whole roads/blocks safe enough communal spaces. Having a laugh. Sure where would you be if you couldn't have a laugh?

Oh god. ? over g/G go for 'g' thinking declamatory, interrogative, exclamatory general whinge to any oul' deity, or perhaps a more direct supplication? I can tell this evolution to book, or part of one or two of those other books I'm supposed to be writing. Where did it all start? Was it my idea? Really had no notion how difficult I was making life for myself in some respects. Seem to remember the recurrence of a parental phrase (particularly maternal) in various guises. "Don't be always doing things the hard way". "Do you like making work for yourself?" "You're always going the hard way about things", etc. Eem, suppose it depends on what you consider hard/difficult, how you ascertain the level of that difficulty. Yes, this was the mode, and aggravated.

Every third word, that would be, that are going, down in from, seeing very announced.

System, a series of 'umbrella' thoroughfares encompassing a myriad of systematic devices. Methodologies irate! Resistance. Lore. Assemble, disperse, reduce, concentrate. Moribund critique of early, decades ago, lecture on—what is the necessary component for tea towels please?

Some days there is no greater silence. Typewriter stops. White machines can whoosh, click, cars pull up, doors bang, dogs bark. A JCB be involved in holes for lampposts. Pressure in the ears a response to lack, settling of fluid, reduction of vibration, profound sensitivity of inflammation.

Later, who snores/that you talking in your sleep? Sneezing, they're sleeping too. Day's debris littering floors, shelves, chairs, benches, stereo, footstools. Shoes, caps, hats, recorders, guitars, CDs, panpipes, harmonicas, bags, books, piano. Piano. Scarves mangled on the lofty tree. Contented sleeping sounds throughout. Heating system winding down. Gentle symbiotic snores. Tidy-up day! Regarding, going to bed.

island life
on the
on an
island life
a life on
a life on
this island life

This island life. Enhanced. Almost all indoor taps run water as a matter of course, that there are taps. More coarsely, indoor plumbing of every type an everyday fixture, rare the new build without the ubiquitous ensuite housing a powershower bath, or jacuzzi.

More water than your great grandmother could have hoped to haul/have hauled in a working day, on tap, running down drains, hardly used, round the clock, day in day out.

This island life. More bathrooms per house than common per road in lots of districts when I was a child. That was the 60s, 70s. Are we any the better for it? Undoubtedly a positive contribution to health, general sanitation, decrease in infant mortality rates. Hesitating to vouch for any great trend showing increases in kitchen/food hygiene. Marble, granite, stainless steel, cookers for this/that—do not ensure good kitchen hygiene, compensate for lack of method, knowledge, practice.

Amber glinting light through water
old glass decanters/stoppers
long gone   fern
creeping   against

wall   fluffing
height

your grandfather's
ability with ferns
career choice
grown out of
reputation
opportunity
chance
fortune
words as
tubular
modules

the wooden floor I spent
  days getting clear
moving changing sorting 3 other

rooms first
reorganize make floor
space   play
    harsh winter days
   spreading out what I'm
working on   space
move think shift discard
sound out   night
covered in a model cricket set
score sheets   marked up
miscellaneous   papers books drawings
remains of research Irish
footballer school project wood
blocks architectural and
offcuts painted/natural
miniature plastic figures bears
people diverse animals nothing in...

That's what happens, you write books, chores lurch. Walking in, out of rooms, ostensibly busy, without any of what you came in for/still with that which you had wished to put away. Talking to yourself again. Drifting inaudibly through language/s, unfolding segments, scenes rhythmical structures. Sifting. Realizing retrospectively three. To write (   ) which way the contraflow?

An elegant silence? C'mon! I mean, what's that? Did it configure before your eyes? Unrequested? Or, more likely, are you moidered by the trappings which visually exert themselves to assert, give impress. That remarkable thing *is* enabling. How a word takes on so, even when it means perfectly well, yet how trite in commerce.

Each bright day beaming each bright day beaming each bright day beaming each.

There was another page, facing me. Rooks on the roof break-dancing on their hobnailed beaks. Electric immersion heater bumbling a distant water movement. Yhrumming. In the distance, there is distance. Evident as light, as placement. Loci. Oh light. That'll have passed [ ] by.

In between your figurative landscapes. A little room for exclusion perhaps? Rocking lightly, slightly leaving, enters the benign affray. There, it's easy. You can do it too, just as an ad for.

Or you could resent the intrusion.

Retrospectively I seem to understand now, what self-preservingly could only be admitted in small, filtered doses then. Yes, there were people trying to tell me. Kind, good, experienced people, who I had known, loved all my life; who had known you for so much longer than I had.

It had to be absorbed slowly. So probable, imminent, did it seem, yet so wrong. Books stopped, waiting, paintings stopped. Everyday attention as always taken up with the mundane to'ings and fro'ings with which we are so familiar/get by. Admittance a multi-layered event. Dredging through many lives, years, uprooting, mixing up, blending, highlighting. Resonances of many perspectives reaching far more deeply than the usual platitudes, however well meant.

So, do I appear to be writing a book about death?
Do I appear to be writing a book about love?
Writing a book about writing?
A book about not writing about core agenda topics?
[Ditto jargon]
Book about people?
About fiction?
So many people are their fiction, it would be unwise to separate them then? Least they collapse into a frighteningly torpid dissimilitude. Not at my best with the thoughtless, the unreasoning, unseasoned, picking rows astride faltering ? dissolving into their own suspension. Intent on achieving some semblance of 'image', credibility, or simply showing off. Scutting lorries would give a measure of one-upmanship with more initiative, courage, panache. Ah, as ever. Picking fights only mildly comprehended on a good day. Giving credence wastes time, effort. On a bad day, let's just say it's not a problem. The béal bocht's self-defensive stance, when do we get away from that? Does

it now pervade every aspect of social living in and around stony island? How far back does it go? An assertion, probably easily traced through families' antecedents as far back as such records go, with, of course, exceptions. They being those who managed to break the cycle of poverty, oppression, morbidity; or were never in it in the first place. Sad lack of any reciprocity/closed off possibilities. Inherent fear, narrowness? Definite yearning, striving for respectability, stamp tramp on your face. Oops you got in the way [If necessary, or as a matter of course, depending( ]. Yes, the tedium of tweedledum, affronted, uptight. Rudely demanding, spoilt child at someone's party wanting presents too, now, (another culture that, close, but from a different mindset. Hospitality, sharing good fortune.) Lack of order. Vindictiveness. Desire to promote dis/misinformation. Egoism's trappings. Definitely never having time for/not entering the tit-for-tat league. What's your problem? Go away and write if that's what you want. If you find you can't or won't, do something else. It's nobody's *fault*. Least of all mine, never having met you before or briefly, in passing. What I do has got nothing to do with what you do, in terms of volition. My decrying cornflakes in favour of, say, porridge oughtn't mean you have to make contact via who/whatever/s because you like to eat them still. What frightens you? Start thinking, mouth closed. After a year or two perhaps return quietly, hope you won't see the need.

A certain ruthlessness necessary from time to time. In order to find, make, be in time, to write. Keep one's sanity, self, out of harm's way. (See above, e.g.).

Brain, labyrinthine, that the inscription of a date in October bearing the digit 2 should lead my hand (   ) to write 1990. Is it portentous? Only if you're stuck in the wilds of alchemy sometime in the 1200s. Is it a date of greater moment, then, than others? So how is emotional intelligence/memory interacting with, I suppose, intellectual/academic memory? Memory as art? Memory as fact? Pushing artefact? Constructs. They destroy the day. Lead us for ever on an uninhibited see-sawing through parks, wastelands. The syllogisms of our time. What is the day? They destroy. An elaborate construct hung on the simple mechanics of movement, light. Its absence. An early response to light, on first waking (in life (in our emoto/minds (even proto?) in brief morning dawn. A big aah! of our tentative burgeoning vocalizations.

Hit or miss. So it's your day. Turn, turnabout. She'll say it had to come once she'd lived long enough. She is pleased, yet unmoved. That objectivity necessary to level the blows, leaven the day light leaves behind. Still, as she sits there, children are taken off the streets of Honduras, shot, for being alive. The Brazilian woman trafficked to Ireland, sold into prostitution, is rescued, no doubt for deportation. The benefactors, implementers, sitting in some cosy suburban pad, replete, some golf-related villa, an upmarket city apartment in x, a country-house bolthole.

How many languages constitute the norm of socio-linguistic dysfunction? Though I had never seen anyone carry a baby upside-down before, least of all an adult, and all in one language only. It left a lasting impression, that first occasion. Sadly, it was only one of many related instances. Occasional incidents as some of the children grew enough to be mobile in their own right. Though I don't think it was seen that way, as a matter of rights, or wrongs.

Morning lode tempestuous summer nub. Wind-scudded whitenesses. Decentred eyes all over. (Focalization?) Cores of silence within throughout the pitch and whine rhythmically cadenced as language attacks declaims intones birds lift shifted along paths blown through sky space the denuded shoots attendant curling or bending under waves weightlessness a momentum of substance palpable air carrying too the unmistakeable stench of newly spread dung.

How could it be a story?
energy supplying service
novel
thanks for any

miles away in the downpour
red plastic crate
jigsaw of roads
pieces of light

African violet wilted some more
edging bright ceramic pot
heavy vehicle   hoarsely

pitched squeak
handbrake on
wet house
mottled water droplets carrying
fine dust still
silting glass streaking
randomly later time was a
construct then which
had nothing to do with me
arches leaves tunnels trees
gradient walls flowers great wide open light spaces
walking through dancing round
going on over yet

at this distance
who can say
what the joke
was or why such
simple humour
could appeal

this letter is in hand and also in chin

wandering on
from my room
should remember leaving
aside afternoon
tea loosely based
on real life it is
not in itself
beautiful urban
waters
spotted gardens
filled hung
who would
come getting
ice-cream

curling
fans low
seductive
catching small
currents
day light
goes
unnecessary
still
quiet

In the midst of this barely controlled chaos sat a tea tray, replete, brown bread, butter, marmalade, tea itself, tray resting on an old worn piece of figured linen which on closer inspection has been carefully darned both sides of the weave, to cover its distress. Presumably preventing any further disintegration for some time. The writing style was curious. An uninhibited assertion of feeling couched in the narrative phrases of a kind of middleclass everyday shop speak. Utilitarian entirely functional as opposed to, say, abstract, poetic, lyrical or even conversational. Now that's funny. After everyday one would have perhaps expected a little conversation. Is that one word narrative then such a framing influence? And even if so, does it or should it preclude a conversational ability? The didacts die hard, scrape the surface, there they leer. I'm telling you, I'm telling you, and you're not telling me. An autocratic demotic. That's the nearest I can come to describing the wholescale effect. Unusual, yes. Cast in familiarity, yes. We'll leave it there.
It appears to be shining straight on the corner, angled light streaking floor. Dull trapezoids stretching higher reaches of wall. The woman, that other life she had, could sit here. I can see how she would be/ have been. Small fire lit on chilly days. A stick, walking-aid nearby. Small pile of magazines, books, puzzles. Audio books from library. Medication close at hand. And company. Company. The singing or the squabbling. The calling or the chatting. News of the day coming in fresh with each person, smell of cold outside air, musty leaves, smoke, fumes, clinging to hair. Breaths of description. Big window. Freedom to move, where, when she wants. Change room. Trick with piano. Look at the back garden, sodden. Dry, fine day, out she goes,

helped to wooden table, chair held ready on gravel, sheltering in the lea. Snapshots of uncertainty. Writers about what is, could be, never has been. Taking a picture using your new piece of technology, you aren't too careful with the set-up light, angle, size in frame or pose. I realize this is because for you it has become something that requires, nay, expects, is a prerequisite to, intervention. Otherwise known as interference. Change. Readjustment.

Tipping the fulcrum. Beautiful early Spring week. Baby birds sang chirpingly down chimneys early morning, mid-day sun blazing, for here, eighteen/nineteen at least, dry, clear.

Young Polish man met his death/was killed, yet to be established. Why? Young men, strong, intelligent, independent, using their initiative or… what?

As eggs is eggs, people recoil, some in pity most in self-defensive horror. Thoroughly understandable reaction. But reaction, not response. Already prevalent, levelled at anyone "Eastern European-looking"— "you're Polish?" Levellers, brands, pigeonholes, ghettos.

Why should an old, dying, invalided woman, of the best, the very best calibre (but what of it, could be, should be, immaterial to the crux of…) have to wait until literally her dying day, twenty four hours, for the necessary, humane level of pain relief? What are our hospital policies on this matter? Why? Where does the budget hit it? Why? Does policy vary in writing/legislative impact or in practice from one health executive administrated area to another? One type of hospital to another? What are their criteria, their justifications?

Maybe you are young, Irish, money in your pocket, bank account, car, house. Lots of holidays abroad, a big mouth (though the two are neither mutually exclusive nor co-dependent). Do you want to be the Polish man? Do you want to be the Russian/Latvian/Croatian/Lithuanian/Slovakian/Serbian/Estonian/Czech/Slovenian/Ukranian who *must* be Polish. Do you want to be the Pole who's being stereotyped so abusively (no dogs, no blacks, no Irish…). Do you want to be the old woman, swelling up slowly, organs closing down, pooling fluid, hurting all over, dying inch by inch — [too ill for too long to be able to speak up for herself effectively so sidelined.] Is this the best we can do for our ill, our vulnerable?

We are all these, more others, will be. Unless we decide to know how our world works, their world works. Affective change.

stars came out
effectually
light transparent
ice
melded edges
glass
whose eye
never missed
beat ear true generous
heart strong song
still long all goes on
continuum
carrying
[we have mentioned before
] propensity
how it does not end [cannot…
readjusts world

adapts grows round moulded impress

restarts sidekicks evokes reflects

no unnecessary largesse

(when you realize you have been waiting
(that you too were waiting

s'always too soon
'course none of it
should ever have happened but will
anyway would have
has this
so imperfect
transience arbitrary to
unfair
wanting remembers
how

vital
sure sound tune time again
down from the line cross henhouse roofs
don't think

it was a
question
catering
whims
permission
fail
lose
fear because
worth features
opinion
permission
to try

baby blackbirds at it
again that high insistent note hunger
cracked shells litter gardens
long
grass robins
egg/speckled/blue
blue lying green
garden
clog literally factually
actually awfully
real jagged
edges fragile
chipping powder
blue

daylight goes
on   sees
walking
reading   laughing
thinking
hurrying
avoidance

knowing all
mutuality
mutability

daylight goes
on   see
walking
reading   laughing
thinking
hurrying
avoidance

knowing
all
mutuality
mutability
surely not
becoming simply
theoretical   just as
never as dubs say
purely biological
how collective 'societal' memory is
short   selective   self reflective
cowl like   (capuchin

well in his seventies   april 1947 bitterly cold hard long winter   severe fuel shortages compounding restrictions   much food rationing still finally lighting coal fire as temperature in living area plummeted to low fifties   imagining an england ahead coal mined out   unable to support beyond 5 million   regressing to agrarianism

in torpid heat august '87   anybody who didn't need money had fled the city read sylvia beach in her paris bookshop   adrienne monnier swathed in pullovers scarves   outdoor jackets   thick lisle stockings sitting on newspaper wrapped in rugs   all heating systems on fuel restrictions   achieving 60 degrees sometimes a good temperature what mean for similar types of north american homes at that time? how much stoicism or lack of   in context   merely a situational reflection of what has been most customary? what conditioning are you bringing here?

            she didn't take that   didn't want to
how many ways could there be (not are there) of looking at such
things?
what if she didn't take in as she didn't need to?
how does that affect the interchange?
does she know?
conscious choice?
or filtering system partially innate/instinctive (suspect debatable
terms whilst restraining from developing new lexical items could
only be another subterfuge   will return to this issue) partially
evolutionary adapting to environmental circumstance?

        you hear   hurdy gurdy
that   chirruping chorus
continual chattering
all over
              filching worms
larvae of biting insects fine earthworms
garden needs them all   ladybirds on
loganberries
could live without hoverwasps
horseflies mosquitoes blackflies bluebottles
could plants as aphids would

if the weighted centre (presuming there is some substance extant in the first place) were to implode what would the natural extension be? how would it look? an uneven splotched spread out mess of? or what? Perhaps it would involve no real incursion into the external world, all exterior factors remaining intact, untouched. Only a severe, permanent explosive dehydration of the internal elements altering its state. The substance would, thereafter, not be any the less substantial than it had heretofore been, maybe. Although any amount of dehydration ought to involve a requisite amount of evaporation therefore probable initial condensation. So a slower transference necessary mutability slow process of exchange. Perhaps, indeed, governed as much by the dimensions of the actual external planes involved as by the prevailing temperature and humidity levels at that exact(ing) time of change.

It could, I see, be a long day. I could take pleasure in this or avoid it.

Either way makes something longer, an attenuated waffling of the day. Faffing about one way or the other.

You could say springing straight towards a night would be preferable, would at least constitute a definite act. Though an act of what intriguing integrity is another matter.

But this will not happen. None of it. Having no desire to control the mannequins or merely react to any of the undeniable externals. So...

We are, tediously, back to square one minus any resolution. Knapsack, bookbasket in tow. Chickpeas steeping. Cut-and-come-again cake too (three types of dried fruit spices sugar tea). Aha tea. To cook is to eat reasonably well. Not to cook is to have debts to cafes, restaurants, pubs and certain large grocery outlets; whilst being hungry, relentlessly, at inconvenient times of day and night. Also, to have rather skinny, angular children whose loud stomachs would, naturally, whine a lot. So, cooking, with bonus compost. Slugs revel embarking on a foray into the produce of our produce's produce. Silly.

So, you can see I'm tired of the slogan type diary style. The relentless propagation of the notion, by large publishers who ought to know better: and that far from being irritated, annoyed, insulted, outraged, offended, disappointed, saddened, upset or etc. by the flogging increasingly of that dead horse of literary styles the pseudo factual, sentimentalised chick-lit/darling mummy style diary writing as base, as narrative hook, as psychological verification of character's female credentials, as, god bless us, literary stream of consciousness; it leaves me cold. I've seen others incensed by it. I regard those books as just another expensive package I don't buy. Neither a personal nor a collective insult. Simply boring, derivative, unimaginative marketing of a very basic, practised, similar style of writing. Not good. So why waste time? Not a contender. That's how hard-nosed it really is if you take away the money out there. So work.

On that note
you can't   often merely you won't
don't   how can you?
          or
          it's not fair
why not a rebarbative which does not provide sufficient rebuttal
I don't think so   clearly mostly no
least we forget   I have decided I am important in this role as
                    spokesperson/representative

that's the end/now
               /of that
               /" "   then   I've decided it's over

Amongst other things realizing I had not had to buy additional soupspoons, the more traditional European rounded ones. These were slightly shorter than average, did not have the deep bowled top I had used in early childhood. Silver replaced by stainless steel, a more modern artefact. They had crossed the country after the death of my aunt in the west and subsequent debilitating strokes suffered by her brother Jack till he could no longer cope alone. He came to us first via a rehab hospital, followed over the ensuing years by an apparently haphazard selection of items from my father's homeplace. A large portrait of grandfather attacked by damp, mould. A set of icing cones, on the dresser to the right, belonged to my grandmother Sarah and auntie May. Their soupspoons, the stalwart remains of their stations and wakes tea service. Was it too modern to have been used at any American wakes? For years a beautiful mink coloured heavy hand knit cardigan, May's last project before her untimely death by cerebral haemorrhage. I finished and wore it with faded out skinny jeans, washed out t-shirt, combat jacket (genuine FCA…) as a young teenager. Though several years waiting to be old enough to do so had wrought moth mayhem on one sleeve which subsequently became a complicated chartwork of darns. There hadn't been enough wool left to knit a new sleeve.
Lists, legacies. Missing people pulling memories up, colliding, realigning parts of   back then
peel carrots, roughly chop, soup in slowcooker.

Thirteen euro. Holds enough for... saves standing stirring switching, remembering, just being there

Is it a revelation this reading of my own handwriting, rapid intricate graphic formation replicating itself beneath my hand relatively distinctly? Reading glasses are useful, should be the least of my worries. Interesting to see some artists make money. Artists make money. Now there's another one of those nicely ambiguous phrases. An ambivalence in practice for some.

A question of intent. Lives lived out as an event for public consumption.

Rationally, moderately, view these aspects, facets of consumerism. Turn all around examining thoroughly, then hold upside down. Does this have immediate or apparent effect on their gravity? In every way. Paint the white face whiter with cardinal red circling widely exaggerated lips, constant muscular grin. Who wins? How much does conventional clown get-up owe to early twentieth century North American society? When was the densely curled wig introduced? The exaggeration of the lips and eyes almost to grotesqueness? Traditional pierrot makeup does not include such distortions or any palette beyond a monochrome base; the introduction of a single hue as shift in register, tone, scenery, prop, focus, a brief focal punctuation in the dynamic play. Dandified elderly andy pandy or andy pandy as a roundeyed anglicised safe baby figure. Circus troupes where clown figures on a par with golly-wog toys of yore. In what media are we informed/offered awareness of that beyond certain early cubist modes or JBY and, rarely, in passing commentary on same? Who notices inherent social signposts overtly? But the stories go on in the plays too, moves, timed laughs, why settle for more? This is easy, too easy. Recalcitrant primitives, refractory race. You've missed Séan's point(s)edness.

Five years. Can it really be? Surely we can permit ourselves wandering as much as resting? Who would say are permitted? That begs the question.
Time is an animal. I am not in charge of any animals. Time is not

an animal. This does not make me in charge of it either. See how to replicate the non-intricacies of the young male American prose writer's wisdom, profundities. Formally he would like to be obscure. Actually, he is a pastiche maker, copyist, perhaps a huge career later as a summarist. Brevity seems desirable thinking of him as such.

What can be seen in this that isn't already known? How can the showing appreciate in mind? How many ways are there to a beauty that is unavoidable, that will recur independently of our deliberate contexts?

Don't fool yourself. You're as deliberate as I am.
Does it matter? Why? Why matter if it matters or not? We are back to likelihood of initiative, wherewithal, response ability, in/dependence and the question inherent in the use of that word beauty in just such a situation. The oul' triangle, went jingle jangle, I remember putting it somewhere in the back of a book when I was younger. It seems I was younger. There were not so many demands, consequences, or I was happily unaware of most of them.

Is it a revelation in the darkened, darkening house? Many words flung about, dynamic mechanics, redemption, suasion, anger, loss, disbelief, hope, despair, fear, order, chaos, joy, all words. Fitting agendas, filling pages, paying bills, lengthening CVs, chalking up notches, adding stars. Political manoeuvres in the dark, consumerism.

Some days there are no efficient words available. Some words reign interminably. Vice versa. Pictures jostling for space. Colour echoing a barrage of silent vibrations. World sprouts. World is, reverberating. Beauty.

The faces of the remaining mingle with those who are gone in more articulate ways than I would have expected. Almost credible, slight contextual warping, shifting. Clarity of such faces etched eyes fleeting expression, meta-language I grew up in, learned to speak in, or not. Such voices practically elusive now. Demands, consequences, responsibilities time. Takes longer to listen so intently. Do it, smile, do it, sing.

This is the first translation
reconciling experience
attempts meaning
ponders indifference
ambivalence
imposing
whose norms
exiled
consider lost
beloved
compelled
to confront

Interrupted by the very real possibility that in a few minutes I will have no water again. Depart to hastily fill plastic bottles and old quart jug at the kitchen tap. The flooding though more minor in scale than they had predicted could occur has still not completely receded. Council workers pump out drains, low-lying sections of fields near roads where the water table was already too high.

So   if this   is
                my job
   or
      the plum
tree   blossom
         blossoms
when   willow takes
      to spreading
      rooks stop
eating
      roof tiles
guttering   fascia
 jackdaws landing
  on cars
when   early bulbs
       bloomed out
    rotting back
       to root

thyme thickening
beneath   wall
mint shooting chives
purple seed heads
configurating   directional
tangents   your lemongrass
unrevived   withering blades
winter brown   waiting
what you knew would come
so   if this   is
my job
waiting for what
you knew
would come
or this   keeping
the unrevived
blades   winter
brown   as thyme
thickens   beneath
the wall
so   if   this is
my job
configurating
directional
tangents
waiting
keeping
what you want goes on
so
if this
my job
is
or this
plum
tree   blossoms
when   willow takes
to spreading on
rooks   stop

eating
roof tiles
guttering fascia
jackdaws landing
on cars when
early bulbs blossomed
out rotting back to
root thyme
thickening beneath wall
mint shooting chives
purple seed heads
configurating directional
tangents your lemongrass

That rabid decontextualization of events in history passed off as specialization that is the past let the future be acknowledgement recognition attempts at just accurate representation pathways out beyond these putrid paltry categories this plethora of squeezed shapes unaligned moments rearranged to serve whatever current political agenda retains enough academic power crucial funding to get away with it who do you serve? Why?

This is what the writer does.

Imagine it
lower calibre critique makers pigeon holers
enough to be that
(there are always alternatives
boxin'
terminology cramping
(after all the alternatives lads
attempting delimiting
proscription seeking
curtailment
bid for?
bounds of?
set by?
strangely reminiscent

rant at
young unfair unjust
hindsight liberal minded
outward bound
those mirroring friends
narcissistic gits' anger
resentment fears institutions
religious secular tedious
orthodoxies whichever
level of whatever hierarchical
order
have that effect
specially over zealous
uninteresting to
whom? me of course now
I'm a narcissistic git see
easily tables turn events
unfolding

So you want it? Get it. Time. Chronic long-term illness many just don't get it, what preconceptions hamper a straightforward thing? Why strive to turn the mundane more mundane? So eminently windable, remind myself not to contribute to the morass with cynical red herrings, obfuscation.

The mystery at the crux of such not what/why, in terms of a life, how: survive, grow, develop, evolve be/love/d see, hear, watch, listen more acutely. Watch out for the vulnerable children, elderly, everyone hears not many listen to. Ageism rampant in this society; always a strong, somewhat fatalistic element especially amongst the poor, deprived. Never the prevalent mode. Very few want to know, do the work, young or old. Not the ambience I grew up in. Rural life where the old were looked after, sidelined occasionally, especially in poorer situations, fewer resources, less time, but as much part of the family, community (that word now used as disparagement, our socio-linguistic inheritance recolouring tonalities, shifting register, how *modern* are we) as anything else. If I nearly lost you there it was intentional, troughs/sinks, milk churns/creamery cans, bunches/ gangs. An urban inner-city setting, vital evolving fluctuating (here we go again) community with, mostly, grannies and granddads as important parts of the fabric, playing a necessary role in the interactive development of young children who lived around. One which has neither been replicated nor continued. Not by any means a good old days scenario, too few jobs, too little schooling, for men and women. Still a functioning thriving way of life, beneficial for the most part to those who participated in it.

Back, what does a writer do?

Looks, hears, watches, listens, pays attention. A writer thinks, waits, analyses, formulates, intuitively feels, reads a lot. A writer explores music, painting, drawing, sculpture, dance, theatre; moves out in the world, notices the quotidian. A writer draws webs of connections, interconnections, highlights relevancies or irrelevancies, plays down one only so far as does not diminish the truth of its context or stumbles into propagandistic dogma etc.

It would break your heart if you let it, all of it. The writer, families, loved ones dying without comfort, the gentler slipping away at home, younger ones from drink, drugs, car smashes, bike smashes, a general wasting.
Make love not war, wasn't that it? (a bit young myself). Make tea, not coffee (make hay while…) make up don't break up. Black and white. Make up for it doesn't work either. Even I can admit that some aims, while commendable, &/ comprehensible, are reasonably unattainable. Make up your own mind. Now that's a point towards clarity. Reaching.

Getting late in the year to still be here, with you, who?   ? are, struggling along pages. Solstice less than a week away. All that endless summer stuff as kids. Why surprised it felt longer? Off from start of June right through to September. Three months, spacious lives. Another living, separate, tenuous relation to school year.

Remember Ric
remember Ric, Tom
Ric's voice carries music care

remember Cid
sharp Cid adamant
Cid tender Cid
true Cid Shizumi
remember Bob
riding intervals
early evening bell
tolls in out those snowy
days funny ease
ah so that's what it's like to
be all grown up if you're...
remember Gael
reading the reading in
the round over the whiffy
attentive alert open assertive
in tune tuning
in the snowy North too
remember Roy
how we all stumbled picked
slid our way back
through the very quiet
Durham night bedded
down bright snow
remember Brian
Bridget how my
Dad nodded off mid paragraph just so
like home

realizing   ambience   code
of manner   way   being not the
superficial napping resemblance
till then hardly noticed taken
for granted in my longtailed clann
when away for years unexpectedly
find home   intonation   hospitality
sharp dry wit   practical unobtrusive
kindness   dynamics of exchange   brought up
short   my grandmother's voice was
that   where I learnt to talk

city   tangency   plane   at the last

remarking
  evening   police
helicopters circling
   generally
new life
back in Dublin
standing
        clothesline
watching   calculating
            where
they were   hovering
ever decreasing
packing up
old trike   football
scattered toys pointing
to lowering sky
something's
happened   they're
looking   or there's
a gathering march

didn't know your son was dead

tedious business
(said to her)
not first time
through fabric warming air
throes
phone
line like this

morning said any hasty struggle where
light's seen shining
briefly torpor
exclusionary rate
of response less
will didn't won't than sheer blah
mudfly at
large immune to stench] chosen
habitat
environmental
waste following an excruciating
excreta of lack
pitched at [exactly] the
wrong point at precisely] the worst
time in [potentially] the most
underminingly stupid
manner that's
how
snow plains rest
hurt eyes
covering what
landscape
presumption
exists
could almost be functioning belief life

take these words   access   review   media
decline in service   costs   in other developments   initiative
leadership   that failure   the expert   continuing   results   establish
risk   engage   attempts to restore   the issue   was still being
considered arrangements will be necessary   the indispensable framework
warning acknowledged   it did not believe   they supported so the moment
comes   however to be guardedly positive there is no going back   so
interested applicants   choose from a huge   range   compromise agreed
it is the place to be   talk to our professional doctors   confidence
creativity   enjoy a well deserved   book now for best   awardwinning
fun   formula   limited availability   new   exciting times   new
experience awaits   anticipated yields   in the region   timing
critical call today   all inclusive how do you spell   due to power
failure   are now poised   as a mark of respect   delivery within 1 week to
capitalise on reservation recommended commercial enquiries   welcome
unprecedented growth only 45 minutes from   nationwide great location
great food   lots to do after renovations   all should be back to normal
by now   see website   subject   to availability   choose from   selection
available now   fill the gap   sudden departure stock arriving daily
awardwinning complimentary car parking is this what we are reduced to
day   light   snow
wind   sky   bird   night
river
abhann   oiche
éan   spéir   gaoth
sneacht   solas   lá
where did these words come from
proto what
is this a series of articulated
sound the youngster hoeing the
small enclosed tillage
would have recognised
not have run from
what has happened to vowels since
slurred encased in Norman French Middle English

embedded   whose lyric tone   chaotic on the   frontline

montbresia   phone
rang   back
now   brain   none of those flowers
long   ago   where   clay paths ran
stone bordered   between banked up beds old kitchen knife
sitting on path   colours surround   dappling light
continual murmuring hum   insect life   tucked away   borders
    sight   plants   swaying   above   casting   delicate
        shade   moving across   lit   page   reading in
    hum   to against with   hum in a fabric   curving
changing   gently impeding   any hasty story   this is how i
weeded   paths   here   grass pile   broken clay rimmed
knife   dirty fingernails   hacked up earth behind
sitting   reading   long time   till
missed meals   struggling up   eyes streaming   through
fabric   scented light   renting the tent   wakening wheezily
cantankerous   clearer light   air humid sense of
river   near

this is conforming to (the predictable, predicat/ory/ing)
expectations (the predatory plagaristic pseudo pluralistics as early
20thC) plastic art

[one could/can/should/would
(always/possibly) change ones opinion

titillating the logically/
suppressed monomania
dogmatism lingering alternately
fingering the controls
apparent
interfering with movements
tinkering at (the) (referentiality)
substantiality referentially
(substance) [(references)
which of course is not acknowledged
respected
accepted
seen
as
given
its head
lights shining reflective pools darkening undulating convex
always seen by pedestrians driving someone else's engine cranking
every shaft roaring visibility which systems remachined in the tiny metal
shell resounding pulsating smelly clustering dark(nesses) hedging
continuously replacing/dispersal of light

only
voice
so
lo'
ice 'd
up on
nerve
eye tock
day rhythms
through

open to light

is it, then, seasonal? what are so many points
climatic attribute those triggers? missed
deigned to evidence jettisoning such is clarity
itself at the flotsam so issue
requisite times effectively or omission
of year
but it didn't snow where do the
nor did i hear though the wind aeroplanes fly?
any song blew

celebrating grieving if we know
what are we
the parallel laid down doing?
tracks others why?
intent action might ?
move us still what is freedom

resonance echoes [besides (a big word

has it affected any
in the world real good
taking turns it seems in life
at being unthwarted even
bereft it was turn a little of
was being how come/ whose impulse
last who didn't
time say [feeling of]
ennui
dreadful
coffee goes cold presuming to know
punctuation marks of day feel
child reads minds enough yet
intuitive would
reaching
post does/does not come touch who
leaving sense of paints /
a smell evocation sky wings

one

It's today. Take a fresh page. How many thousand words? It's a laugh. Take a fresh page from the pile. Recycle. It's today. The clouds down, mist, steaming up off the bogs. Even the magpies don't go out. There were seven perching strategically on Saturday. We haven't seen any of the young blackbirds since.

The mist may meet the low cloud cover. Imagining Mount Brandon, shrouded smelly with summer moulds, gullies and potholes invisible, lurching straight up behind mist. Will o' the wisp.

Ceaseless noise of white machines. There are some constants beyond this. Not enough to look for more, other. Not enough to decide to quit. Not enough to say not enough. What if? Silly session ensues. Disliking this type of irrationality posing as imagination, nostalgia. There are books full of it everywhere.

Baking to go, making dough. One hundred years ago the same. The one I know without having to look up. My hands, after years away from this particular activity, take off in a rhythmical series of sequential movements each designed to fulfil a certain function necessary to the act of breadmaking. My head wanders through layers of thought while processing sudden vivid visuals that pop up in time, it seems, with my hands. It's soothing, restful, satisfying. Tasty. I learned this process from two or three, assistant to my grandmother, in the new store, the room that opened off the back of the ancient dairy. It contained a waterwheel which had been used to run the churns, rows and rows of wooden shelves along the stone walls for apples from the orchard. The flour bin, a large oblong wooden chest from which we took all we needed to make the bread, except the buttermilk which was in the dairy. We worked on a long three-sided wooden 'breadmaker' tray, which went back into the chest after.

The window was a small Georgian French door affair, casement style, through which I clambered to the summerhouse to play, or to check on the sluice gates for the channels from the old mill race. At that time we regularly still let water through onto the immense wheel behind the outdoor toilet which effectively sluiced everything out several times a day. Quite a clever system. Not one I've come across anywhere else yet. This I knew as a working relic of the past in an era when many homes still did not have indoor toilets or bathrooms, and in some cases nothing outdoors either, beyond a pit in a shed or a bucket in a back yard.

Bread. Bread and butter. The things I learned stuck. Standing on a little wooden stool by the buttermaker (high, wooden workbenches with a slight slope, built-up sides) busily working my butter pats, slapping and shaping, beads of salty water squidging out of the pound of freshly-churned farmer's butter as I knocked it into shape, reducing its water content. The ridged paddles, allowing me to start patterning an intricate series of checks on the surface as I shaped it, though I also liked to wield a smooth paddle and on achieving an even, passable block shape to use one of the more decorative devices; small carved wooden forms which impressed their design on the smooth damp salty butter. Ready to be wrapped in greaseproof or waxed/oiled paper and carefully packed in boxes or baskets, depending on whether they were going by train (Dublin) or "to town", locally. I liked butter. Still do, but none of it tastes the same.

I liked the churn and the separator too. I've written about them before, here and there. These are not only memories, but functional processes which with some hesitancy and mistakes, I could actually make work again, in the right circumstances. Not to mention frame of mind. Butter is responsive to how it is handled. There are lots of other people round the country who could still remember enough, of watching, doing, helping, to do such things. Before we all forget, have lost the art. After thousands of years of butter, even in the bog, preserved, why should we give up so easily? Cowed by money. Cramped by modern circumstances. Rendered obsolete, outmoded by commercialisation.

June 1st 2004. Tuesday. A reaching forwards/backwards into that non-thing called time. Truly a non-entity. Cheap pen from a shared hotel room stuttering out its ink parsimoniously, presumably designed to ensure none of the complaints on the accompanying cards get too long. Hard to be erudite, in a hurry, with an annoyingly faulty pen. Self-censorship. Circumstantial. Bound by context occurring in collusion with, or opposition to, all the other facts. Which one, what? Pieces of information, extraneous detail, parallel coincidences. Events in suspense, dynamic, powerful. Having a "pull", a "wake", a glitch on the lip of surface viscosity.

Air, we know it's there. Humid, still. Wet, moving. Arid and laden. We in the world watch air spread, revive, remove, resume, as if it were nothing. So accustomed are we to it, so much do we take for granted its presence that we have grown, effectively, to pretend we are immune to it, or that it is not necessary. We have so much we do not notice. We have so much we do not care. As long as it's there our major institutions and governing powers cannot see it. And we comply. Why does everyone have to be so "good", so compliant? At precisely what age do we start the sad process of blinkering our young children?

That pen is irritating me. Back to essentials. Writing with the refill minus the useless plastic trappings. Does it slow me down? Inevitably. Is that a bad thing? Which way is the wind blowing?

This time we all grow up learning to pay too much attention to. Light I understand. Darkness too. Even the abstract mechanics of the sundial I can accept as a funny thing to do with light and rotation. Light, its absence, movement. These are the metronomic features of our days. The language of time. How fast can you fly? Does that make you any more beautiful than, say, the swift? Any more happy than you were ever likely to be?

I am writing a book of words. I have written books of words before. Sometimes I draw and paint, make things, contraptions, devices, objects, clothing. Cook things, grow things, alter and reuse things. Paint walls, fix cars, teach children. Play music, attempt to look after sick and elderly, nurse family. Edit, proofread, guide. A long line of diverse students tutored, lots of paper qualifications thrown in, none of them mine. Chief facilitator, cynical but (one hopes) just arbitrator, giver of grinds and remedial support. No wonder I'm so bloody tired. That's only about half of it.

Many things, occurring, contemporaneously, vogue of whinging seeping the groundwater of our social culture, why? That solid, permeable bedrock relied on, envisioned when far away, abroad, alone, eroding over 30 years or more.

The leaching process has perhaps irreparably changed the more traditional Gaelic modes of social interaction, particularly over the last ten years. As if somebody were giving, throwing away, ancient heirlooms whose provenance alone made them interesting, beautiful, and hence once so prized.

In return, as in the fifties, sixties, seventies, they were happy to have (though having to pay up) a formica-topped table, a gas cooker with cylinder, (the ubiquitous 'kosigas'), an elaborately framed pair of sunglasses (60s), pilot's shades (70s), raybans (80s), police glasses (90s), etc. Now it's cheap electronic gadgetry, accessorized to the hilt of conformity. A logical extension would perhaps be a choice of vertical blinds or traditional Venetians for your mobile/pc screen, quickly followed (as colours and designs run out) by the new, quirky lace curtain option; perhaps with pink Barbie logo'ed ribbon tiebacks. That would be a neat marketing fix, wouldn't it?

After all, that *is* the age group at which so much gadgetry, logo'ed branded clothing, toy and junk food marketing is aimed.

Advertising. Don't start. This is where even my seventy eight year old mother reaches for her soapbox. Her particular dislike, how poor quality, cheaply produced food is marketed and presented to children. She is right. Elitist foodism is an old chestnut, heavily tied to issues of ethnicity, religion, socio-economic, socio-cultural, and socio-political class. The culture, so endemic everywhere in the world, of bullying by exclusion does not need any further bolstering. The medical statistics available on heart disease, high cholesterol, strokes etc don't either.

"Think outside the box", "imagine", "innovate", "promote a new, previously non-existent framework". Just some of the banal clichés of our current times in the western world. Where "think outside the box" means "create" an analogous situation, make a paradigmatic set of assumptions and pin everything to those, call them "new" even "innovative". Miss the wood for the trees, deliberately? After all, lots of people, being paid lots of money to show they can prove the formula, turn it on its head, or inside-out, issuing disclaimers whilst pulling a rabbit out of a hat. So many industries require so many labourers. Gradgrindian. Utilitarian. Class-ridden inequalities of race, gender, learning modes, religion and all the usual etceteras.

We in our world are still a long way from throwing off what we think we have already rid ourselves of so emphatically. We are, everywhere, such a short time as industrialised cultures. How stupid to have thought, presumed would imply the process more accurately, that we had advanced way beyond anything our Victorian or Edwardian forebears knew, or had to deal with socially. The same problems rear their ugly heads all over the world on a daily basis. Hunger, starvation, disease, poverty, debt, homelessness, racial, sexual, and religious persecution and discrimination, torture, institutionalised abuse/torture, arranged marriages, "forced" marriages, domestic violence, child prostitution, poisoned water, poisoned land, poisoned air, war, both civil and "international", the many ruled by the few, inevitably, "jobs for the boys", political corruption, financial corruption, infant mortality rates always much higher in minority groups (as with clinical medical conditions), deforestation, the desertification of previously arable land, religion of one kind or another as the panacea of the poor, the socially acceptable "respectable, educated" face of crowd control, vote-canvassing, and electioneering of all kinds. The loss of whole languages as the few associated with more economic power suck in more immigrants, tie up more loose ends in the accreditation systems of educational institutions, demand their language be that of commerce and international trade. This is not new colonialism. This is very old, traditional, unchanged. Ask the modern Aztecs or Maya, their ancestors slave labour on their own land, denied all human rights, including their own language. Or in reference to such a situation previously the norm here in Ireland, to quote the Limerick poet Michael Hartnett

"finding English a necessary sin
the perfect language to sell pigs in."

These matters are not just still within living memory or oral testament here in Ireland as in so many parts of the world, they are a crucial determining factor in how people choose to interact socially, what they aspire to attain, how they use language and how they view language.

Watching and listening for many years, carefully taking note. There I am. Seeing language used from a perspective of it being an entity entirely in its own right, outside the speaker. Between the speaker and the listener, objectified. Held up to close scrutiny. This can be a useful block. A solid structure, independent of either party, capable of deflecting as much as hitting home. Ready to be turned on its ear or at an obtuse angle, if so required. Obfuscation. Precision. Humour. Let-outs. Fall-backs. Formulaic modes. Mind and ear attuned to this several hundred year old game of pass, I got you! Fluid rapidity alongside careful slowness, parity in motion.

Much needed and campaigned for policies of social inclusion and equal rights are being implemented here via government departments and the public sector. These essential changes to institutional policy are still in their infancy in terms of real-time application in this country. Progress is being made, it is, of necessity, evolutionary and not always clearly visible in practice. The shape of progress in any such field is essentially non-linear, multifaceted and multilayered. Incidences of homelessness throughout the country are appalling. Provide more respite shelters, and long to mid-term hostels as in London, for instance. The money is in the country, use it on the people who most need it. Provide and adequately fund ongoing research and implementation of training and provision for all categories of "at risk" school children. Lower the commencement qualifying age for access to resource teachers and support staff to school entry age, or better yet preschool year. Provide state funded preschool daycare for every child. Fully subsidized for those who could not otherwise afford it, and means tested comprehensively after that. Let it be as "free" as possible and available to all who want it.

Provide ante-natal and post-natal outreach clinical services in community based settings; GP surgeries, community centres, parish halls etc. The level of non-essential medical intervention in childbirth in Ireland is appalling. Wonderful having a highly rated, world renowned maternity hospital in Dublin, shame that unpublicised policy across the state is that of the baby factory and that our hospitals are not clean enough to be safe. There is lots of money to be made in that particular industry. Provide a fully functioning and supported midwifery scheme including domino effect liaisons between midwife, GP, hospital and gynaecologist, with full post-natal follow up and continuity of carers a priority. Available to all, not as an expensive designer shopping option.

Neither the manner of airing and criticising any of these issues nor the few suggestions made are in any way new or radical. This opportunity is used to draw attention to them because there is so much room for improvement. These are not glossy media-friendly topics on which all people feel well-informed currently. Sideways related topics crop up once in a while, but there is no evidence of even an everyday understanding of what one's rights are in areas pertaining to such issues, or even of what is commonly available and accepted as a norm for best practice in other European countries. Now what possible reason could there be for not disseminating this information to people in the street? Why have we not heard more about media censorship in present-day Ireland? The only nod in that direction is the by now ubiquitous wink at the tip of well-known party political affiliations of certain newspapers, usually brought to our attention in the run-up to elections and at times of political crises. So little as to be hardly worth mentioning.

one landscape
on the face of it
seems to have the
edge of the scene
cleaner or the director
outlines what he has
in mind the locations

alluded to travel
happily the natural
world corruption and
failure

why not?
you can
pretty standard
qualify
she wrote to me

walls are what happen

odd details emerge
it was an insult
the inhabitants
sheep
with high profiles
sometime in '95
that occasionally
admit to being confused

I noted this down

ironically

a media wit
a media with
a media width
was eventually
disqualified

off the back of
acceptance attention
turned to who
meanwhile verge
on the slightly uneasy
style there's usually
a fact and readers
would last pleasure
enthusiastically

it was a few weeks ago

expertly calibrated
propped round the
walls

the throes orchestrated

but

real begin
site approval has
finally been settled

sort out access

ruin
remastered

it'd be interesting to know
on the night

veneer
no longer
the hardest circumstances

he's been working with
irreconcilable polarities
on the basis of
nothing sweet'n'sour tangless
and with followers

to gather in afternoon a plain day
book
as i was thinking this name forget
out of the blue change sky morning
first rain breaking across swept
treetops now it has come
tame
predictable mute rather wet
remaining rosemary bough
drenched wagging too far
window box crocus pansies
wild primrose fuchsia juniper small bright
arrows out
stormed all night
rented house new
doubleglazed windows perhaps
just left there
air
-ing no mould
unmoved ringing changes
no lark in sight
one or two here
over three and a half years good
average? a mean

certainly paucity
on the ground

and rather chilly
i doubt
lunch
unidentifiable
believe myself for joy

dustbins
it's snowed cold

it ended all the women sitting silent

had the brightest
made up most
my mind considered shades
overslept best
day began i could do trying
so happy keeping up
the storm o gladsome we left
light travelled
sat rustic far together
summer house back so young

till alfriston echoing tones of left talking
summers past like grandmothers
day began overslept
joy
quite dark of it all
awakening from
vivid
quivering dream wonder
singularly distributing for a symbol
morning spent cooking
washed worked moving

images
remarkably familiar
maladjusted nonsense

if angry so ought
we know
each
other

atonal
intonation
tonal
banalities
formal
crass

signed undersigned co-signed
designed even resigned

—a vast similitude interlocks all—
well, not quite

worse, interrupted

still used the old route
back hospital grounds turned
into dead ends finding a way
out between stakes through
broken down benches hedges
derisive there was so little
canal

[to be sure I had not wasted my time here] end of Optic Verve
a commentary

www.ingramcontent.com/pod-product-compliance
Lightning Source LLC
Chambersburg PA
CBHW031153160426
43193CB00008B/351